MILITARY TECHNOLOGIES

TECHNOLOGY DURING THE KOREAN WAR

HEATHER C. HUDAK

Checkerboard
Library

An Imprint of Abdo Publishing
abdopublishing.com

ABDOPUBLISHING.COM

Published by Abdo Publishing, a division of ABDO, PO Box 398166, Minneapolis, Minnesota 55439. Copyright © 2017 by Abdo Consulting Group, Inc. International copyrights reserved in all countries. No part of this book may be reproduced in any form without written permission from the publisher. Checkerboard Library™ is a trademark and logo of Abdo Publishing.

Printed in the United States of America, North Mankato, Minnesota
102016
012017

Content Developer: Nancy Tuminelly
Design and Production: Mighty Media, Inc.
Series Editor: Rebecca Felix
Cover Photo: AP Images
Interior Photos: AP Images, pp. 5, 16, 17, 26, 28; Getty Images, p. 8 (bottom); Shutterstock Images, pp. 5 (inset), 19; USMC Archives/Flickr, p. 12; Wikimedia Commons, pp. 4, 7, 8 (top), 9, 11, 15, 21, 23, 24, 29

Publisher's Cataloging-in-Publication Data

Names: Hudak, Heather C., author.
Title: Technology during the Korean War / by Heather C. Hudak.
Description: Minneapolis, MN : Abdo Publishing, 2017. | Series: Military technologies | Includes bibliographical references and index.
Identifiers: LCCN 2016944855 | ISBN 9781680784121 (lib. bdg.) | ISBN 9781680797657 (ebook)
Subjects: LCSH: United States--History--Korean War, 1950-1953--Technology--Juvenile literature. | Technology--United States--History--20th century--Juvenile literature.
Classification: DDC 951.904--dc23
LC record available at http://lccn.loc.gov/2016944855

CONTENTS

A DIVIDING LINE

The Korean War was three years of battle sparked by a political conflict that still exists. This war actually began at the close of another. **World War II** ended in defeat for Germany and Japan in 1945. At the time, Japan ruled Korea. The peace terms called for Japan to give up control of Korea.

The United States and the Soviet Union were to temporarily occupy Korea. Both nations agreed to a dividing line across Korea at the 38th parallel. The Soviet Union **supervised** land north of the line. The United States supervised land south of the line.

US troops travel through Korea on September 8, 1945, days after the end of World War II.

MANCHURIA

Vladivostok

Mukden

Peiping

NORTH KOREA

1

Pusan

SOUTH KOREA

Yellow R.

Osaka

Nagasaki

An August 1950 map shows the 38th parallel separating North Korea and South Korea.

The Soviet Union supported communism. Communist **dictator** Kim Il-Sung took power in North Korea. The United States had a **capitalist** form of

5

government and did not support communism. **Capitalist dictator** Syngman Rhee took power in South Korea.

Tension grew between North Korea and South Korea over their different types of government. On June 25, 1950, North Korea took action. North Korean troops, or the Korean People's Army (KPA), invaded South Korea.

The Soviet Union supported the KPA in their attack. The United States requested that the **United Nations (UN)** defend South Korea. On June 27, the UN asked member nations to join the fight.

US ground troops arrived in South Korea on July 1. Including the United States, 21 countries came to the aid of South Korea. At first, their goal was to get North Korean forces out of South Korea. Over the course of the war, their aim became to unify Korea under a non-communist government.

During the Korean War, both sides used a combination of both established and newer, more advanced **tactics**. Jet-powered aircraft were a major development during the war. And helicopters were put to new and important uses. They acted as **ambulances**, quickly carrying injured

UN and US troops trained South Korean soldiers in military tactics before and during the war.

soldiers to safety. This meant more soldiers survived their injuries to return home.

The war continued for three years, ending in a signed **armistice**. This put a stop to the fighting. But the disagreement over government and leadership continued. More than 60 years later, the Korean War has not officially ended.

TIMELINE

JUNE 1950

On June 25, North Korean forces invade South Korea.

SEPTEMBER 1950

US forces defeat the North Korean army at the Battle of Inchon.

JULY 1, 1950

The first US ground troops arrive in South Korea.

OCTOBER 1, 1950

South Korean troops cross into North Korea.

JULY 10, 1951

Armistice discussions begin between the two sides. However, terms are not agreed upon and fighting continues.

OCTOBER 25, 1950

China launches its first offensive of the war.

JULY 27, 1953

The two sides sign an armistice agreement.

2

ON THE GROUND

The first invasion and early battles of the Korean War were fought only on the ground. Soldiers met face to face in armored **vehicles** and carrying small arms. Many of the weapons used by both North Korean and South Korean troops had been developed during **World War II**. These included the M1 Garand, a **semiautomatic** rifle. Soldiers also carried smaller, more lightweight M1 carbines and Browning **automatic** rifles (BARs).

In addition to small arms, both sides used **mortars** and **howitzers** in ground combat. They also used tanks. These tough armored vehicles carried soldiers, had mounted guns, and could travel through all types of **terrain**.

South Korea obtained US tanks to fight against the KPA's Soviet tanks. One was the M4 Sherman tank. It was lightweight and moved well through Korea's mountain landscapes.

When US troops joined the fight in July 1950, they used M26 Pershing tanks. These **vehicles** had heavier guns and better armor but were less trustworthy. One of the most popular tanks of the war was the US-made M46 Patton. It was heavier than the M4 and had a more powerful engine than the M26.

M9 rocket launchers were powerful handheld weapons made to battle tanks. The United States began using

them during **World War II**. Soldiers most often held these weapons on their shoulders. Upon fire, a 3.5-pound (1.6 kg) rocket was launched up to 500 feet (150 m). These explosive rockets could penetrate a tank's thick, metal armor.

At the beginning of the war, South Korea had fewer weapons and soldiers than North Korea. During the war, it continued to gain **artillery** and soldiers from supporting nations. This brought on a new phase of fighting. Both sides battled from trenches and launched massive amounts of artillery at one another. Neither side was able to gain and then keep the advantage.

BATTLE OF BLOODY RIDGE

Bloody Ridge is a group of three hills that lie north of the 38th parallel. Beginning August 18, 1951, North Korea and South Korea, aided by UN troops, began a weeks-long battle there. North Korean troops had created a series of trenches on the ridges of these hills. The trenches could hold as many as 60 soldiers. Within them, the northern troops were able to effectively hide from enemy fire.

However, these steep hillsides were a disadvantage in wet weather. Rain turned them into slippery slopes. This made it difficult for North Korea to bring in more troops and supplies. After weeks of fighting, South Korean and UN troops overtook the ridge of trenches. Thousands of soldiers had died on both sides. The series of hills became known as Bloody Ridge.

TRENCHES ON THE BATTLEFIELD

Trenches were holes and tunnels that soldiers dug into the earth, often in hillsides. They provided shelter and cover from enemy fire. Soldiers fought from trenches, hid in them, and stored supplies in them. Some trenches were so deep that soldiers needed a ladder to climb out of them. Others were large enough to drive a truck through!

⌦(3)⌧

HARSH ENVIRONMENT

Korea's geography presented great challenges to ground troops. Much of Korea is rural and mountainous. Soldiers traveling through mountains became easy targets to enemies hiding on peaks and ridges.

In addition, it was difficult to get tanks, **mortars**, and **howitzers** through narrow mountain passes and up hillsides. Getting supplies into rural areas was a challenge too. Mules and human porters were often used to bring soldiers the supplies they needed.

During battle, US and **UN** troops would surround an enemy on three or more sides in mountain passes. Then they would fire heavy **artillery** to keep the enemy from escaping. This **tactic** was known as a flash fire.

Troops needed to dig into the ground to set up gun mounts for flash fire. But this proved difficult in Korea's **terrain** and seasons. Many of Korea's valleys are rice **paddies**. In summer, these paddies were too wet and soft

US troops forge through North Korea, where the terrain is more rugged than in South Korea.

to hold up the mounts. In winter, the wet ground froze, making it very hard to dig into.

The Korean climate was hard on soldiers as well. Temperatures could reach 100 degrees Fahrenheit (38°C) in summer. In winter, they could drop as low as –30 degrees Fahrenheit (–38°C). The US government developed special cold-weather uniforms for the soldiers to wear.

The uniforms were made from natural fibers such as cotton and wool, and were layered. For the first layer, a soldier wore cotton underwear and a T-shirt. He often also wore long johns. Over that, he added a **flannel** shirt, sweater, pants, and a woolen vest.

The next layer was a coat and pants made from water-**repellent** cotton. This kept out the wind and rain. Finally, a long jacket was layered on top. It was lined with many layers and had a hood to

US troops in white uniforms that provided winter camouflage. Winter snowstorms were common in North Korea.

add extra warmth. The soldier wore leather gloves with wool inside.

Soldiers' uniforms were also designed for camouflage. Winter outerwear was white to blend in with the snow. Summer uniforms were camouflage print, green, or brown to match the landscape and surrounding plants.

4

IN THE AIR

In order to gain an advantage on land in Korea, ground troops needed support from the air. The United States knew from **World War II** the importance of having control of the skies. During the Korean War, it employed many aircraft. These included jet-powered fighters that engaged in head-on battles in the skies.

One of the most common jet fighters was the F-80 Shooting Star. It was the first US combat-ready jet-powered aircraft. Its first military mission was during the Korean War. During the conflict, the F-80 was replaced by the more advanced F-86 Sabre.

Both the Sabre and a Soviet aircraft called the MiG-15 changed the way wars were fought. These planes were more deadly than any planes before them. They were faster and more **agile**.

TECH FACT

Head-to-head battles fought between jets in the air are called dogfights.

A MiG-15 performs in a 2010 air show. More than 15,000 of these aircraft were built between 1947 and 1957.

The Soviets had about 2,000 jet fighters involved in the Korean War. Most were MiG-15s. These heavily armed jets could reach a speed of more than 620 miles per hour (998 kmh). They could climb quickly to altitudes of more than 50,000 feet (15,240 m). These superfast jets took US troops by surprise.

Shooting Stars were no match for MiG-15s. The MiG-15s could fly higher than Shooting Stars. Shooting Stars carried machine guns or small rockets. These weapons were not as powerful as those used by MiG-15s. However, the Shooting Star's weapons could be fired at a faster rate than that of the MiG-15.

At first, the Sabre was also no match for MiG-15s. But the skill of US pilots usually provided them an advantage in battle. So, even in areas where the MiG-15 had performance advantage, US pilots won a majority of head-to-head battles.

Over time, American engineers improved

TECH FACT

A Sabre's machine guns could fire about 1,250 bullets per minute. A MiG could fire between 400 to 550 bullets per minute.

the Sabre. By 1953, this aircraft was superior to the MiG in nearly every aspect.

Throughout the Korean War, more than 1,000 pilots flew US-built F-86 Sabres.

F-86 SABRE

The F-86 Sabre was first used by the US Air Force in 1949. It later became the primary jet fighter used by US pilots in the Korean War. The Sabre held one pilot, who operated the aircraft and its weapons.

1. When a Sabre pilot took to the skies, he first used radar equipment to search the sky for enemy planes. This radar could find a target up to 30 miles (48 km) away.

2. The pilot's radar scope was located in the cockpit. Once a target was located, a **blip** appeared on this **technology**.

3. The pilot locked the radar onto the target. This activated a computer in the cockpit. The computer then determined a **collision** course.

4. The pilot followed the collision course set by the computer.

5. When the plane was within 20 seconds of the target, the **automatic** tracking went off. This signaled to the pilot to prepare to fire. He entered into a computer the number of rockets on board he wanted to fire. Then he pulled a lever called the trigger to fire the plane's weapons.

6. The aircraft's weapons aiming system determined when the plane's stored rockets would launch. It waited until the range was right, and then fired. This took just seconds.

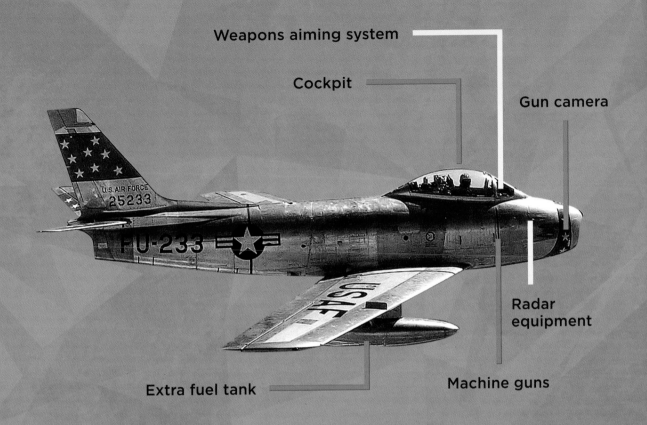

Weapons aiming system

Cockpit

Gun camera

Radar equipment

Machine guns

Extra fuel tank

7. Sometimes the pilot fired at enemy aircraft using the Sabre's machine guns.

8. The pilot sat in an **ejection** seat. In the case of too much damage from enemy fire, he could eject from the cockpit.

5

MOBILE MEDICS

Fighter jets weren't the only air **technology** used during the Korean War. Helicopters were also vital. They were used as air **ambulances** during the war. This use became very important, especially in combination with other medical technologies.

The Bell H-13 Sioux was one type of helicopter used for medical purposes during the war. These aircraft were lightweight and fast. They reached speeds up to 105 miles per hour (169 kmh).

These aircraft had a stretcher located on either

MASH medics rush a wounded soldier from a Bell H-13 Sioux.

HEARTBREAK RIDGE

The Battle of Heartbreak Ridge lasted from September 13 to October 15, 1951. It took place in the hills of North Korea, near the 38th parallel. Enemy troops hid in trenches along the ridge's steep slopes. UN forces fought to take control of the ridge, but failed.

UN forces suffered about 3,700 casualties during the battle. About 1,500 of the wounded were taken from the battle to a nearby MASH. Of the wounded, very few died at the mobile hospital. This is thanks to the helicopters' quick transport and the ability to perform major surgery at the MASH. These technologies saved many lives after Heartbreak Ridge, and that of many more soldiers during the war.

MASH AND HELICOPTERS ON THE BATTLEFIELD

side of the cockpit. Each stretcher could carry one wounded soldier. This marked the first time in war history that soldiers could be quickly evacuated from battlefields by air.

Soldiers were trained to help fellow injured soldiers as best they could until help arrived. Then, the wounded soldiers were evacuated. Helicopters would carry them directly from fighting zones to Mobile Army Surgical Hospitals (MASHs).

Helicopters could pick up soldiers from nearly any type of situation or landscape in Korea. This included from boats, on mountainsides, and even amid enemy fire during battle.

MASHs were made up of tents that held full hospital units inside. They had everything doctors needed to perform surgeries. This included beds, tools, medicines, and even blood for **transfusions**. MASHs could be easily moved to new sites as needed.

The role of helicopters was critical to success at MASHs. However, these aircraft were used for more than just medical evacuation during the war. Some were used to pick up fighter pilots whose planes had been shot down. Helicopters could also carry supplies in and out of remote areas that were difficult to access.

Remote, mountainous areas also made communication difficult between troops. Helicopters were used as eyes in the sky. Pilots communicated with ground troops to give them an idea of what conditions lay ahead. These pilots could also spy on the enemy and pass messages between groups of soldiers.

TECH FACT

*M*A*S*H* was a popular US TV show that aired in the 1970s and 1980s. It was about military surgeons in the Korean War.

6

ARMISTICE

For the first year of war, the North and the South gained the advantage back and forth. In September 1950, US forces defeated North Korean troops at the Battle of Inchon. On October 1, South Korean soldiers crossed into North Korea. But by October 25, China came to North Korea's aid, attacking the South Korean army.

In July 1951, US leaders began peace talks. Fighting continued as the talks started and stopped over the next two years. Finally, on July 27, 1953, an **armistice** was signed.

US Colonel James C. Murray and UN representatives met in Panmunjom to discuss an armistice in October 1951. This village is on the border of North Korea and South Korea.

Armistice talks began on July 10, 1951. An armistice was signed 2 years and 17 days later.

This was not a peace agreement, but one to stop fighting. Korea remained divided. A new boundary was drawn near the 38th parallel.

Much of the **technology** used during the Korean War had been used in previous wars. But the ways it was used in Korea greatly affected the war's outcome. Many soldiers were saved by the advances in military medicine, such as MASHs. These units were employed in future wars, leading to more lives saved.

Jet-powered fighters were key to gaining an advantage in future military air battles. Helicopters also remained important, especially for medical evacuation. These technologies would inspire future advancements in combat and survival **tactics** and equipment.

GLOSSARY

agile — able to move quickly or easily.

ambulance — a vehicle that carries sick or injured people.

armistice — a pause in fighting brought about by an agreement between opponents.

artillery — large guns that can be used to shoot over a great distance.

automatic — moving or acting by itself.

blip — a dot on the screen of an electronic device.

capitalist — relating to an economic system where businesses compete to sell their products and services.

casualty — a military person lost through death, wounds, or capture.

collision — when two things come together with force.

dictator — a ruler with complete control who often governs in a cruel way.

eject — to remove from inside something. This action of being removed is called an ejection.

flannel — a soft cloth made of wool or cotton.

howitzer — a large cannon with a short barrel.

mobile — capable of moving or being moved.

mortar — a large cannon used to fire shells high into the air.

paddy — wet land in which rice is grown.

repellent — the quality of being able to keep something away.

semiautomatic — moving or acting partially by itself.

supervise — to watch over or take care of something.

tactic — a method of moving military forces in battle.

technology (tehk-NAH-luh-jee) — machinery and equipment developed for practical purposes using scientific principles and engineering.

terrain — a particular type of land.

transfusion — the injection of blood from a healthy person into the body of another person that is injured.

United Nations (UN) — a group of nations formed in 1945. Its goals are peace, human rights, security, and social and economic development.

vehicle — something used to carry or transport. Cars, trucks, airplanes, and boats are vehicles.

World War II — from 1939 to 1945, fought in Europe, Asia, and Africa. Great Britain, France, the United States, the Soviet Union, and their allies were on one side. Germany, Italy, Japan, and their allies were on the other side.

WEBSITES

To learn more about **Military Technologies**, visit **booklinks.abdopublishing.com**. These links are routinely monitored and updated to provide the most current information available.

INDEX